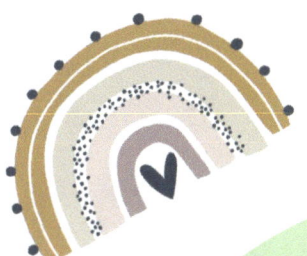
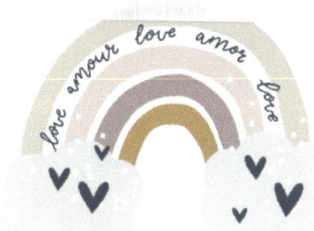

This Journal was inspired and dedicated to My Awesome daughter and son, Justin & Michelle. Love, Mom

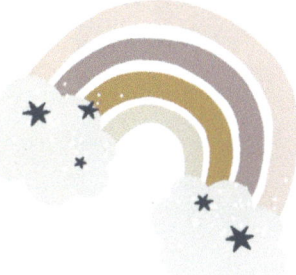
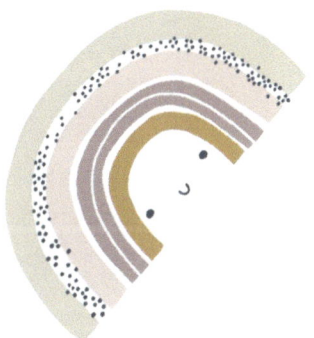

Copyright © 2019
by Cathy's Creations
Cover Design by Cathy's Creations
All rights reserved. No part of this book may be reproduced without written permission of the copyright owner, except for the use of limited quotations for the purpose of book reviews

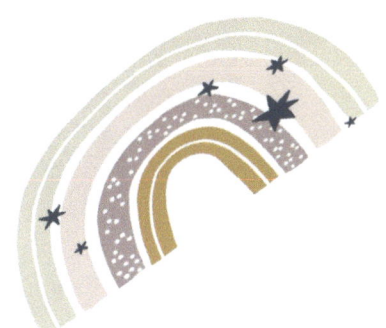
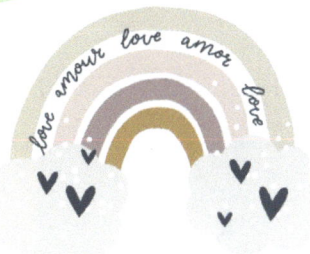

BABYS First YEAR

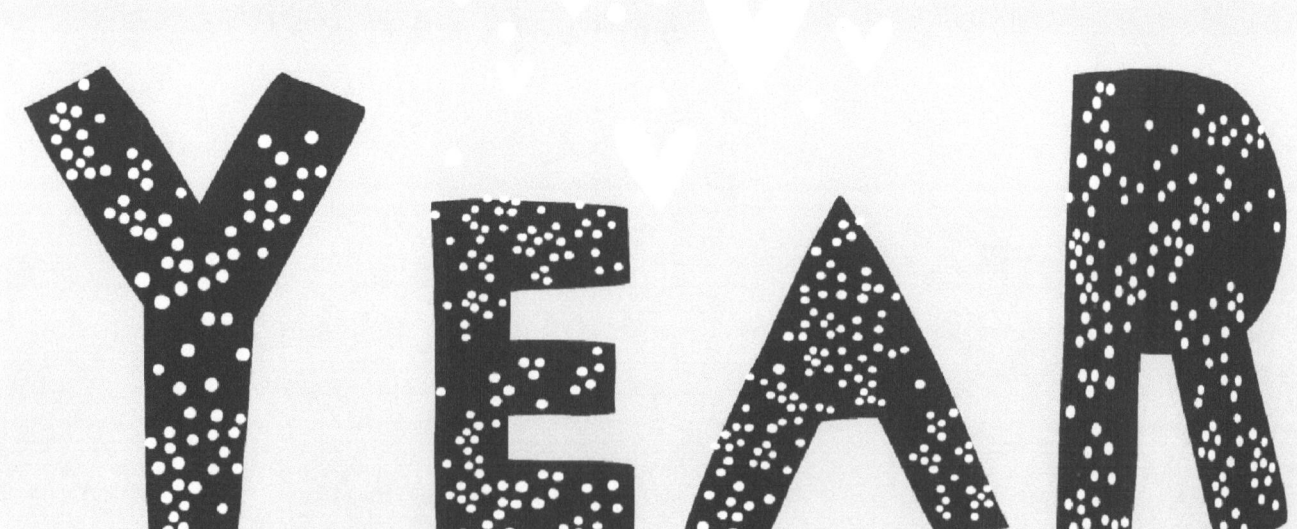

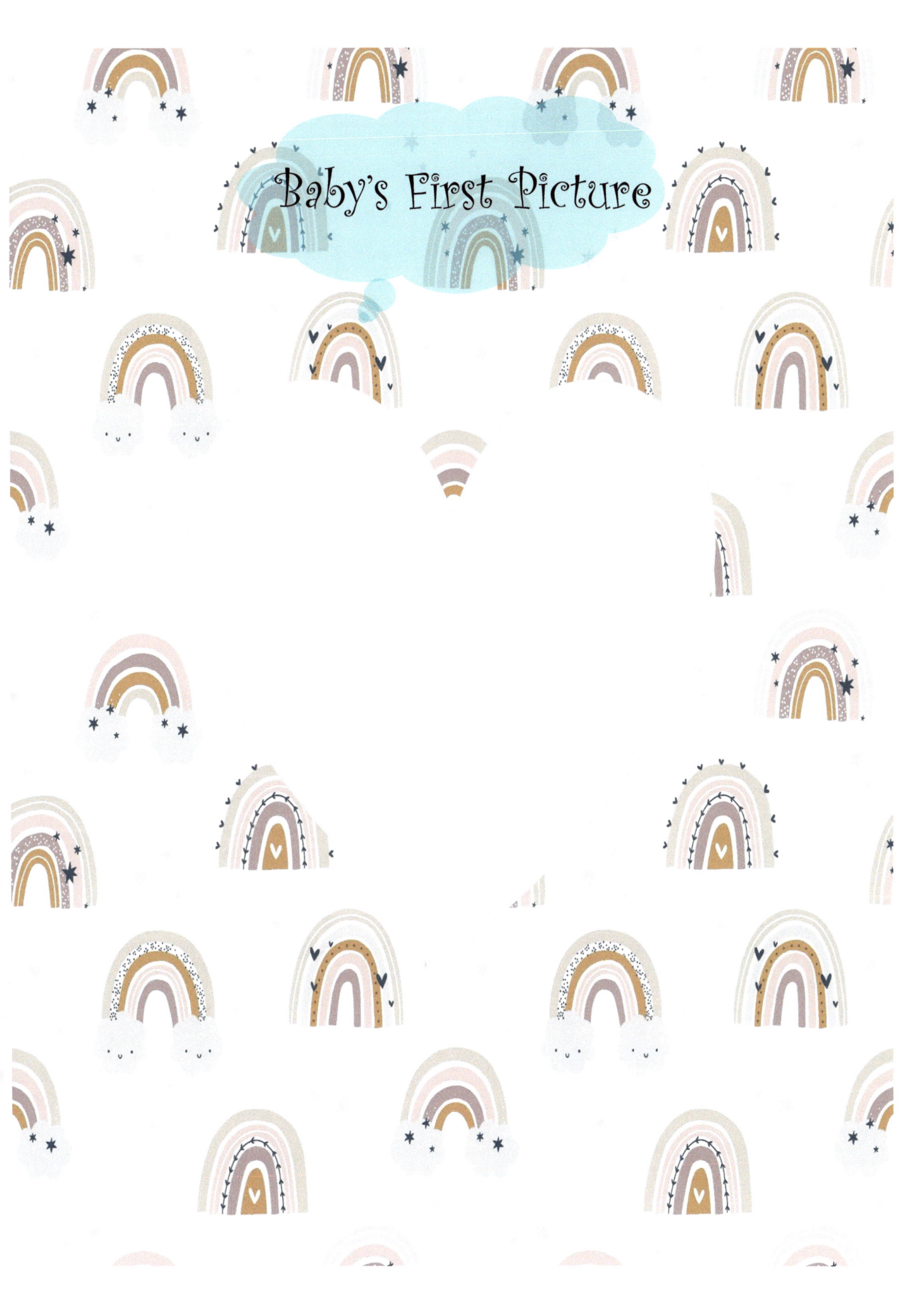
Baby's First Picture

I'm A: _____

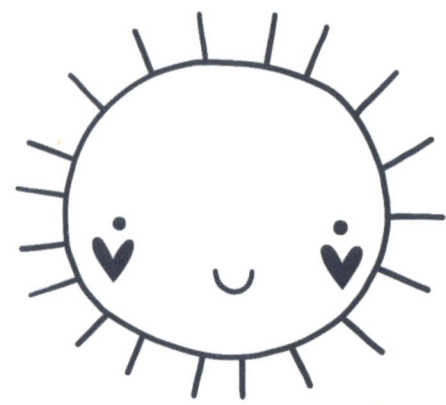

Name:	
Date:	
Time:	
Hospital:	
Weight:	
Height:	
Head:	

A _____
P _____
G _____
A _____
R _____

Delivery Notes

_____
_____
_____
_____
_____
_____
_____

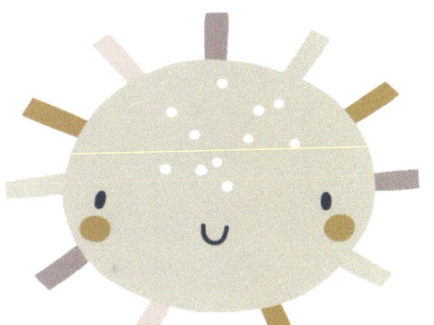
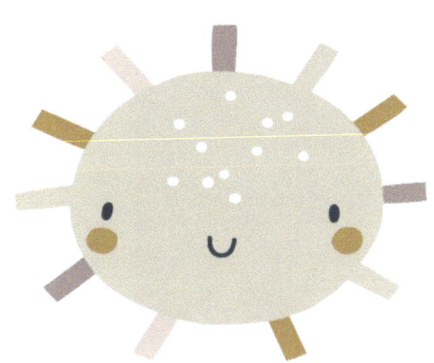

All About Me

Name Options My Parents Had For Me

_____

_____

_____

Eye Color
_____

_____

_____

Star Sign
_____

_____

Hair Color
_____

_____

_____

_____

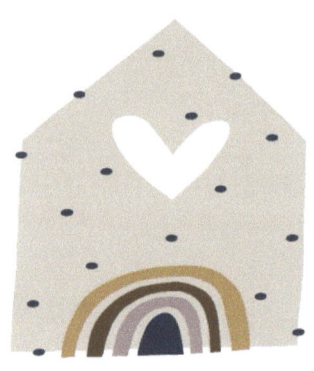
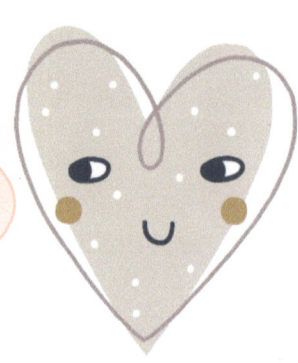

Mother And
Baby Hospital
Bracelets

Thoughts

1 Month Old

Date: _____

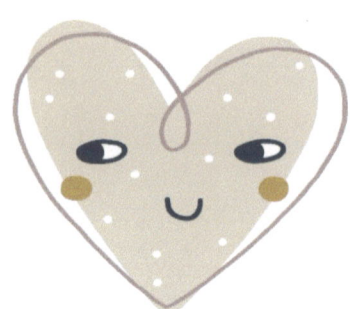

Dislikes

Likes

_____

_____

_____

_____

_____

(Picture)

Weight: _____

Height: _____

Diaper Size: _____

Notes

Sleep Patterns

_____

_____

_____

_____

1 Month Old Milestones

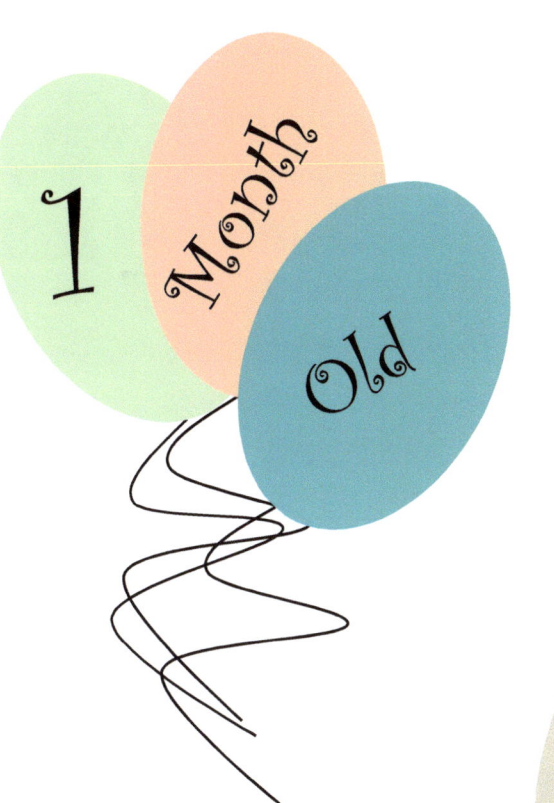

Milestone Achieved	Yes	No
Notices Faces		
Sees Bold Patterns		
Recognizes Primary Caretakers Voice		
Begins To Coo		
Moves Head Side To Side		
Starts Holding Own Head Up		
Brings Hands To Face		

My Daily Routine

05:00

05:30

06:00

06:30

07:00

07:30

08:00

08:30

09:00

09:30

10:00

10:30

11:00

11:30

12:00

12:30

13:00

13:30

14:00

14:30

15:00

15:30

16:00

16:30

17:00

17:30

18:00

18:30

19:00

19:30

Thoughts

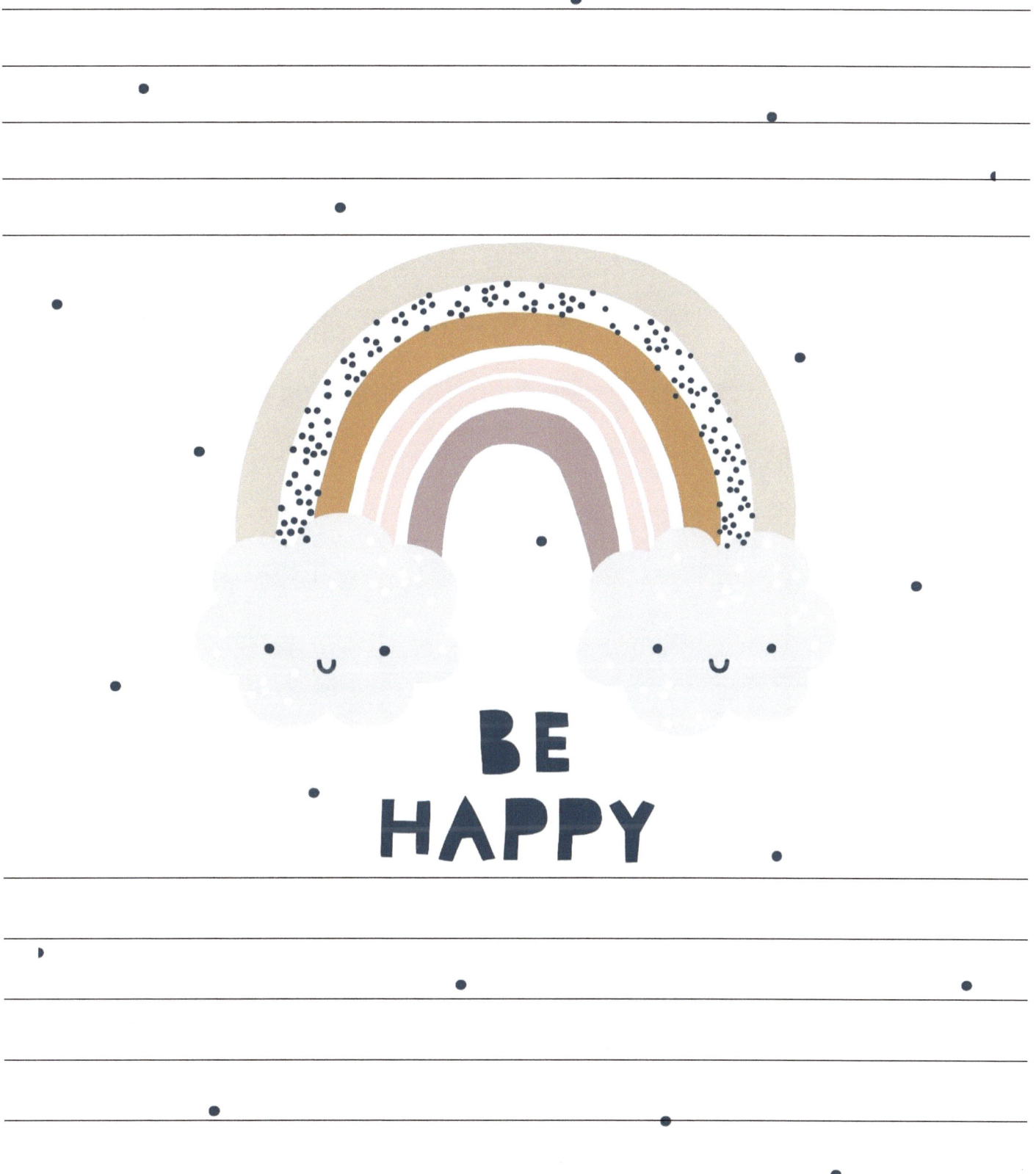

2 Months Old

Date: _____

(Picture)

Weight: _____

Height: _____

Head Circumference: _____

Sleep Patterns:

_____
_____
_____
_____

Feedings:

_____
_____
_____
_____

Likes	Dislikes

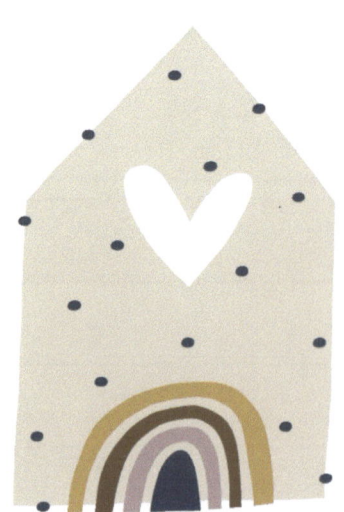

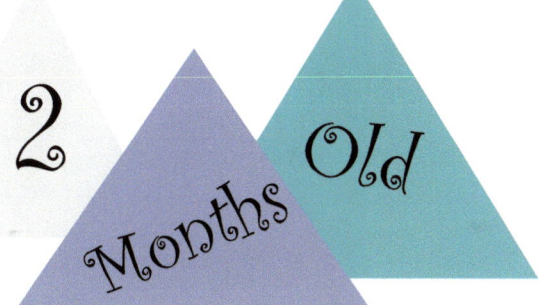

Milestones

Milestone Achieved	Yes	No
Begins To Smile		
Can Briefly Calm Self Down		
Begins to follow things with eyes and recognizes people at a distance		
Can Become Fussy And Bored		
Holds Head Up With Little To No Support		
Begins to push up when lying on tummy		
Makes smoother movements with arms and legs		

Comments

_____
_____
_____
_____
_____
_____

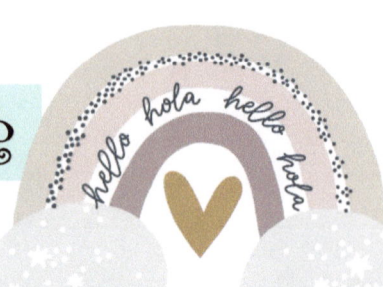

My Daily Routine

05:00

05:30

06:00

06:30

07:00

07:30

08:00

08:30

09:00

09:30

10:00

10:30

11:00

11:30

12:00

12:30

13:00

13:30

14:00

14:30

15:00

15:30

16:00

16:30

17:00

17:30

18:00

18:30

19:00

19:30

Thoughts

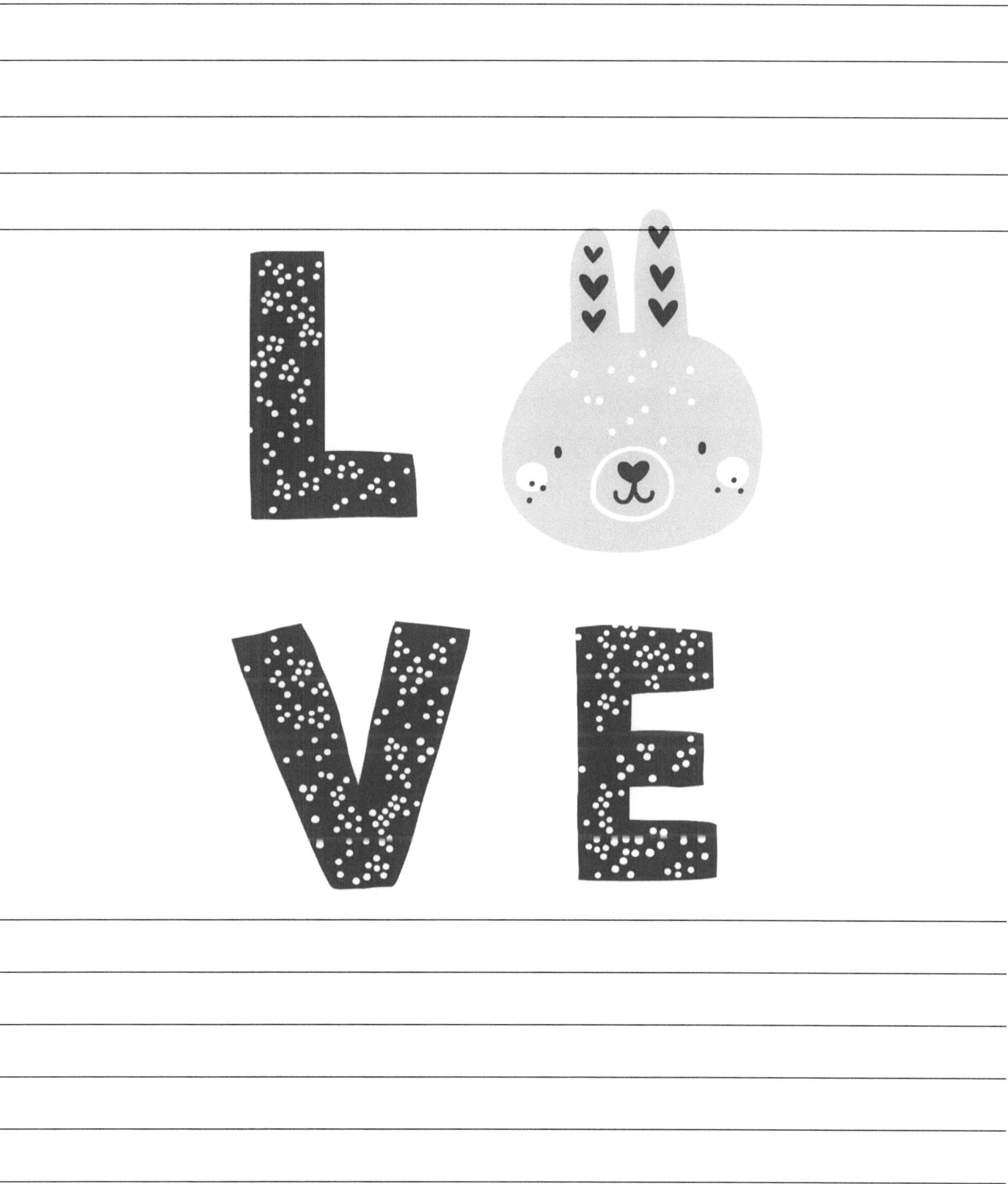

3 Months Old

Date: _____

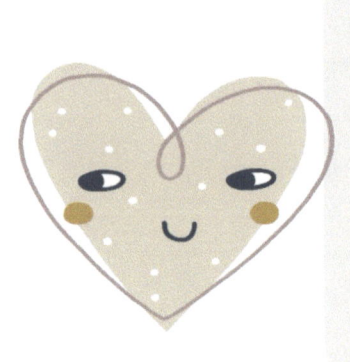

(Picture)

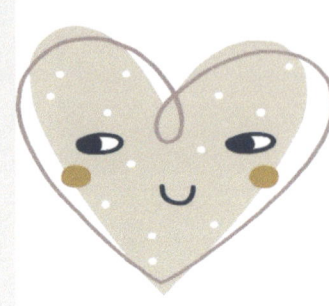

Sleep Patterns:

_____
_____
_____
_____

Weight: _____

Height: _____

Head Circumference: _____

Feedings:

_____
_____
_____
_____

Likes	Dislikes

3 Months Old

Milestones

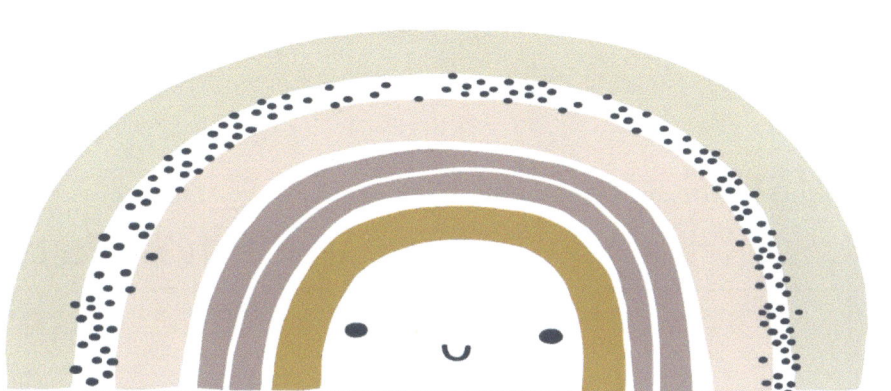

Milestone Achieved	Yes	No
Can Identify Parents Faces From Others		
Starts To Have Different Cries For Different Needs		
Turns Head Away To Express Lack Of Interest		
Opens And Closes Hands		
Swipes At Dangling Objects		
Turns Head In The Direction Of Sound		
Enjoys Playing With People		

4 Months Old

Date: _____

Sleep Patterns:
_____
_____
_____
_____

(Picture)

Feedings:
_____
_____
_____
_____

Weight: _____

Height: _____

Head Circumference: _____

Likes	Dislikes

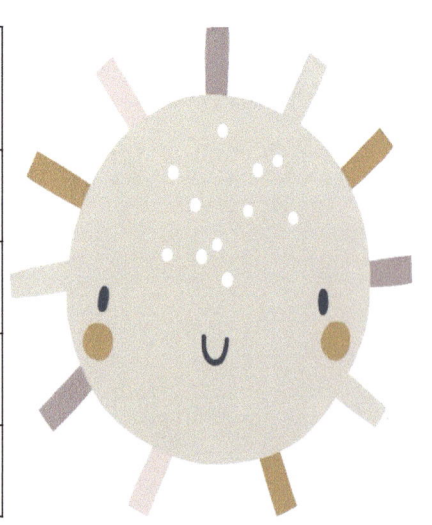

4 Months Old

Milestones

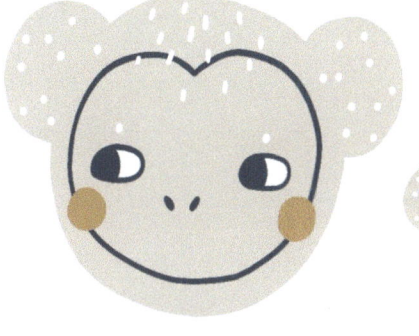
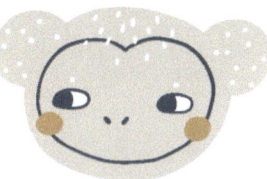

Milestone Achieved	Yes	No
Starts To Giggle		
Mimics Facial Expressions		
Reaches For Toy With One Hand		
Holds Head Up Completely Unsupported		
Pushes Up On Elbows When On Tummy		
May Begin Solid Foods		
Sleeps Through Few Nights		

5 Months Old

Date: _____

Feedings:

_____
_____
_____

(Picture)

Weight: _____

Height: _____

Head Circumference: _____

Sleep Patterns:

_____
_____
_____

Likes	Dislikes

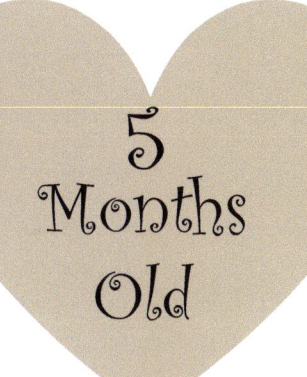

5 Months Old

Milestones

Milestone Achieved	Yes	No
Rolls Over From Tummy To Back		
Puts Object Inside Mouth		
Babbles		
Fascinated By Mirrors		
Begins To Entertain Themselves		
Begins Laughing		
Enjoys Peek-A-Boo		

Comments

_____
_____
_____
_____

6 Months Old

Date: _____

Likes	Dislikes

(Picture)

Sleep Patterns:
_____
_____
_____
_____

Feedings:
_____
_____
_____
_____

Weight: _____

Height: _____

Head Circumference: _____

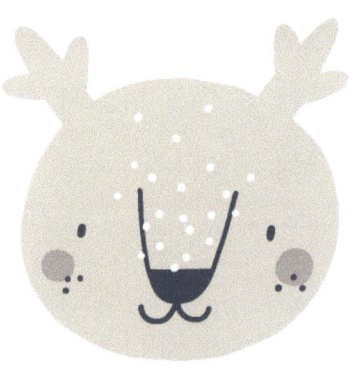

6 Months Old Milestones

Milestone Achieved	Yes	No
Starts To Pull Self Along The Floor		
Fully Starts Solid Foods		
Passes Objects From One Hand To The Other		
Responds To Their Name		
Fully Sits Unsupported		
Sleeps Through Most Nights		
Starts To Understand Simple Words		

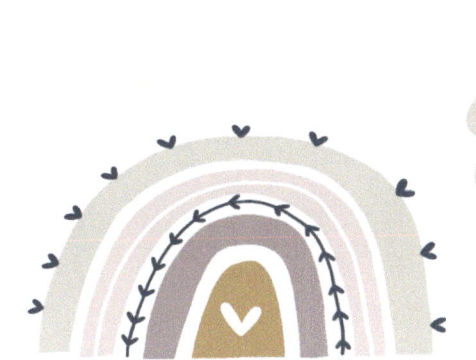
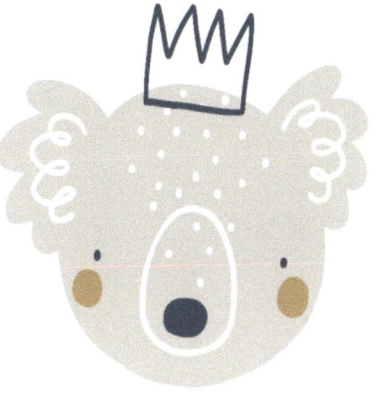
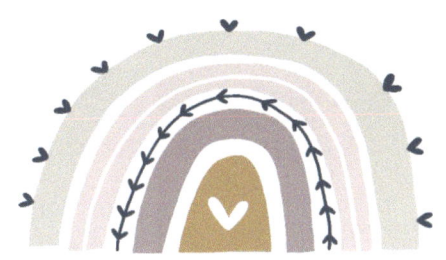

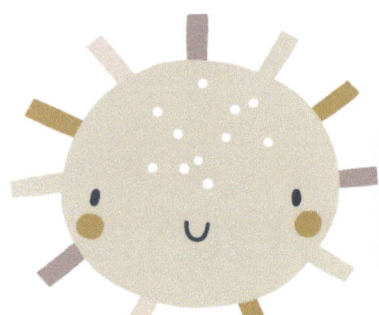 # My Daily Routine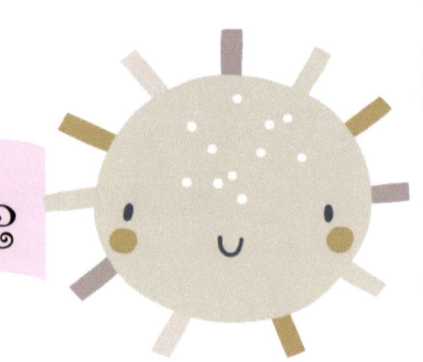

05:00	12:30
05:30	13:00
06:00	13:30
06:30	14:00
07:00	14:30
07:30	15:00
08:00	15:30
08:30	16:00
09:00	16:30
09:30	17:00
10:00	17:30
10:30	18:00
11:00	18:30
11:30	19:00
12:00	19:30

Thoughts

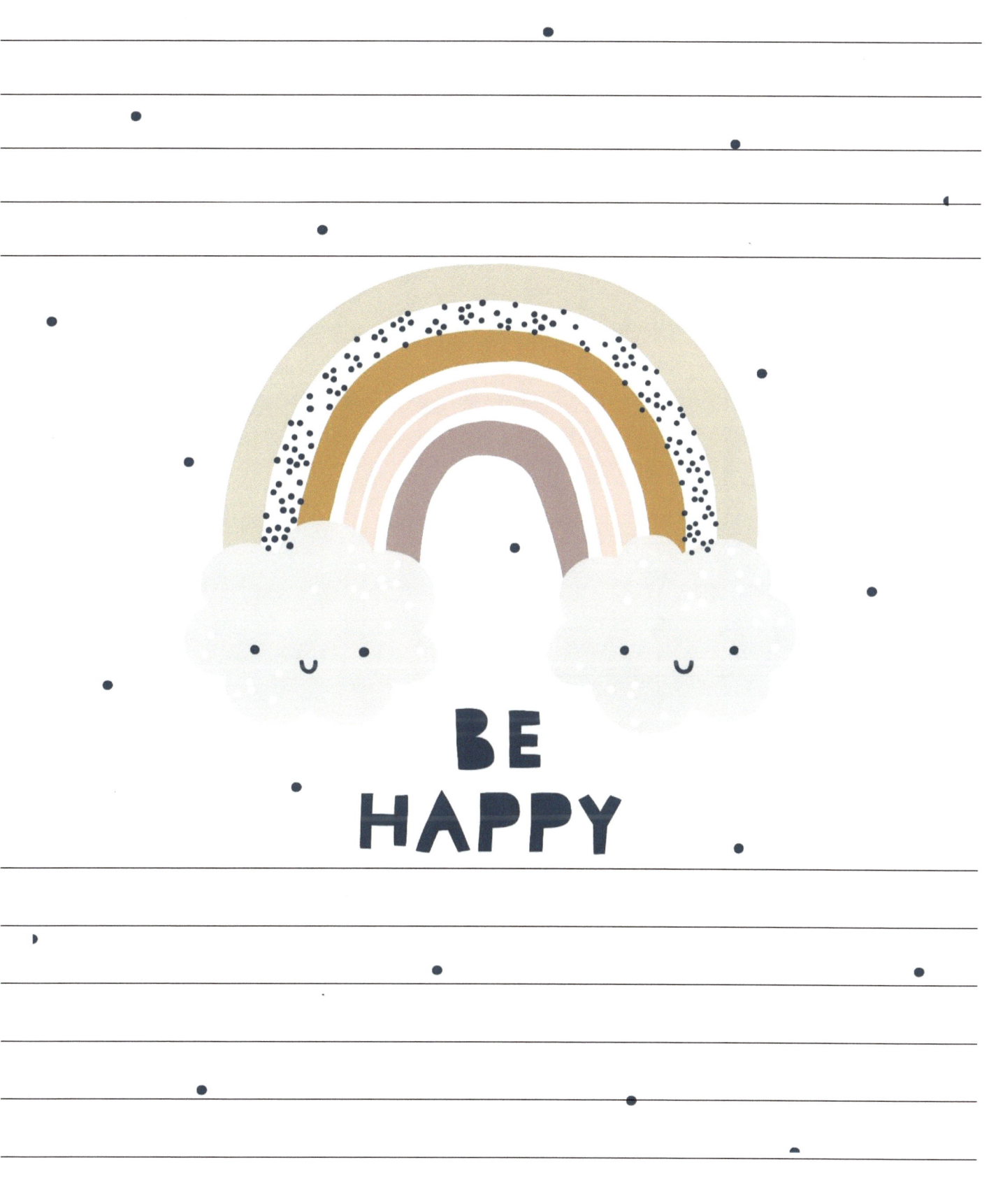

7 Months Old

Date: _____

Weight: _____

Height: _____

Head Circumference: _____

(Picture)

Likes	Dislikes

Feedings:

_____

_____

_____

_____

_____

Sleep Patterns:

_____

_____

_____

_____

_____

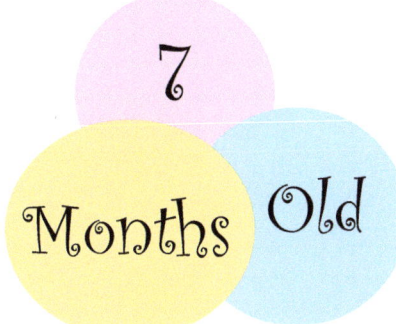

Milestones

Milestone Achieved	Yes	No
Enjoys Throwing And Dropping Toys		
Responds To No		
Enjoys Company Of Parents		
Fascination With Eye Contact		
Finds Slightly Hidden Objects		
Attempts To Copy Sounds		
Bears Weight On Legs When Held Upright		

Comments
_____
_____
_____
_____
_____

8 Months Old

Date: _____

Sleep Patterns:

_____
_____
_____
_____

Weight: _____

Height: _____

Head Circumference: _____

(Picture)

Likes	Dislikes

Feedings:

_____
_____
_____
_____
_____
_____
_____

8 Months Old — Milestones

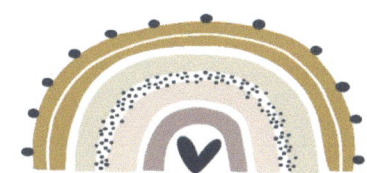

Milestone Achieved	Yes	No
Begins Crawling		
Reaches For Objects Without Issue		
Enjoys Colorful Objects		
Feels Textures		
Stands While Holding On To Something		
Leans To Reach For Toys		
Can Sleep Through The Night		

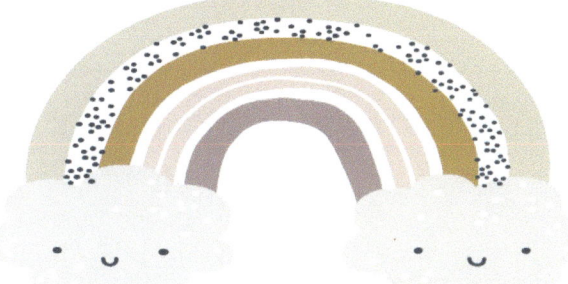
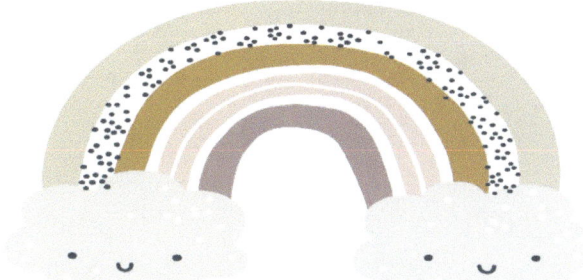

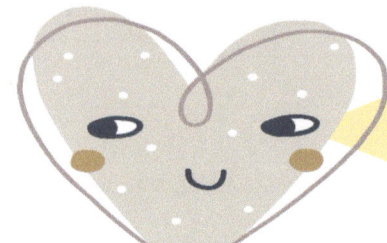 # My Daily Routine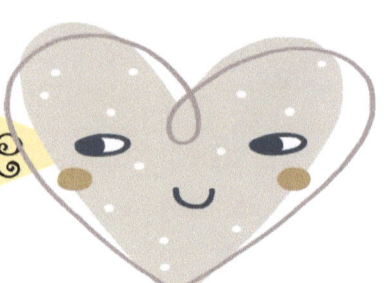

05:00	12:30
05:30	13:00
06:00	13:30
06:30	14:00
07:00	14:30
07:30	15:00
08:00	15:30
08:30	16:00
09:00	16:30
09:30	17:00
10:00	17:30
10:30	18:00
11:00	18:30
11:30	19:00
12:00	19:30

Thoughts

9 Months Old

Date: _____

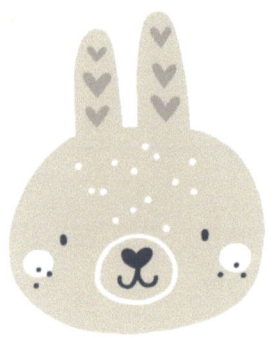

(Picture)

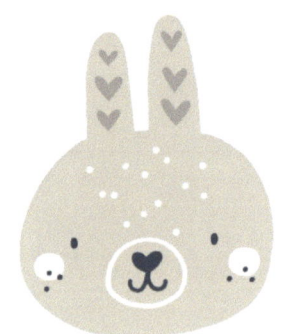

Weight: _____

Height: _____

Head Circumference: _____

Likes	Dislikes

Feedings:

_____
_____
_____
_____

Sleep Patterns:

_____
_____
_____
_____

9 Months Old

Milestones

Milestone Achieved	Yes	No
Becomes Wary Of Strangers		
Clings To Familiar People		
Begins To Point		
Mimics People And Sounds		
Has Favorite Toys		
Babbles And Coos		
Naps Less		

Comments

_____
_____
_____
_____

Date: _____

10 Months Old

Feedings:

_____
_____
_____
_____

Sleep Patterns:

_____
_____
_____
_____

Weight: _____

Height: _____

Head Circumference: _____

Likes	Dislikes

(Picture)

10 Months Old Milestones

Milestone Achieved	Yes	No
Explores Shaking, Banging And Throwing		
Begins To Cruise Across Furniture		
Pulls Self Up To Stand		
Loves Feeling Textures		
Better Hand-Eye Coordination		
Finger Feeds Self		
Enjoys Affection		

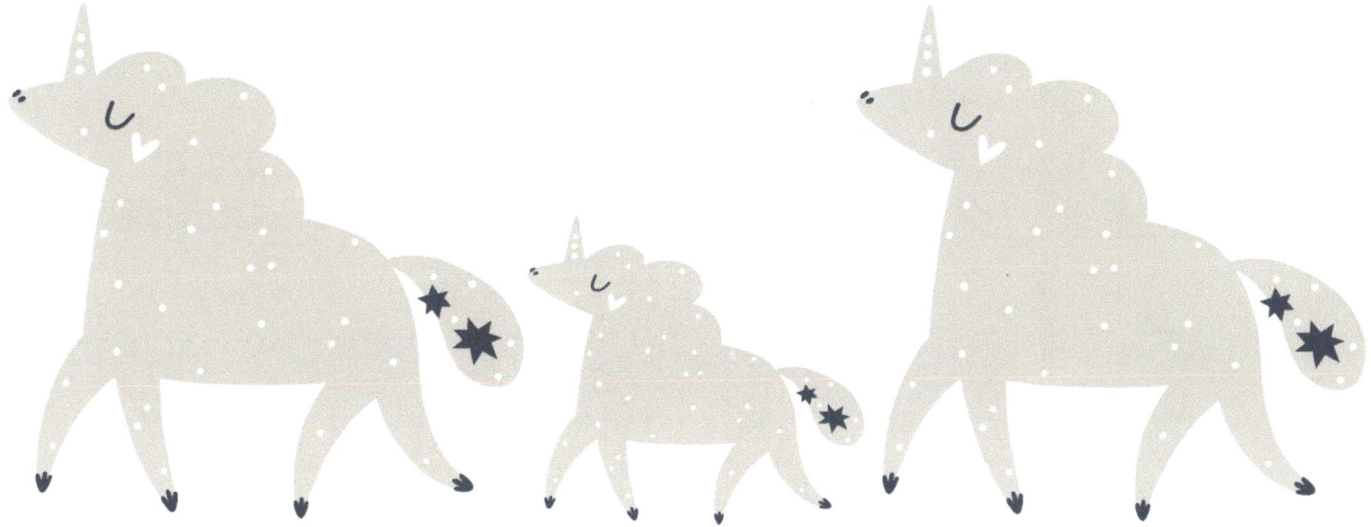

11 Months Old

Date: _____

Weight: _____

Height: _____

Head Circumference: _____

(Picture)

Likes

Dislikes

Sleep Patterns:
_____
_____
_____
_____
_____

Feedings:
_____
_____
_____
_____
_____

11 Months Old

Milestones

Comments

_____
_____
_____
_____
_____

Milestone Achieved	Yes	No
Can Crawl Up Stairs		
Makes Sounds That Sound Like Words		
Becomes Interested In Screens		
Develops Separation Anxiety		
May Be Walking Or Starts Taking Steps		
Enjoys Finger Foods		
Becomes Interested In Books		

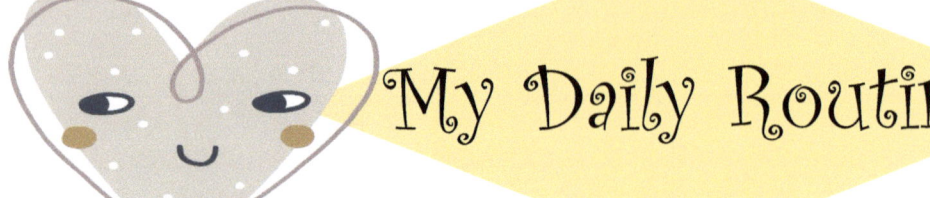

My Daily Routine

05:00	12:30
05:30	13:00
06:00	13:30
06:30	14:00
07:00	14:30
07:30	15:00
08:00	15:30
08:30	16:00
09:00	16:30
09:30	17:00
10:00	17:30
10:30	18:00
11:00	18:30
11:30	19:00
12:00	19:30

Thoughts

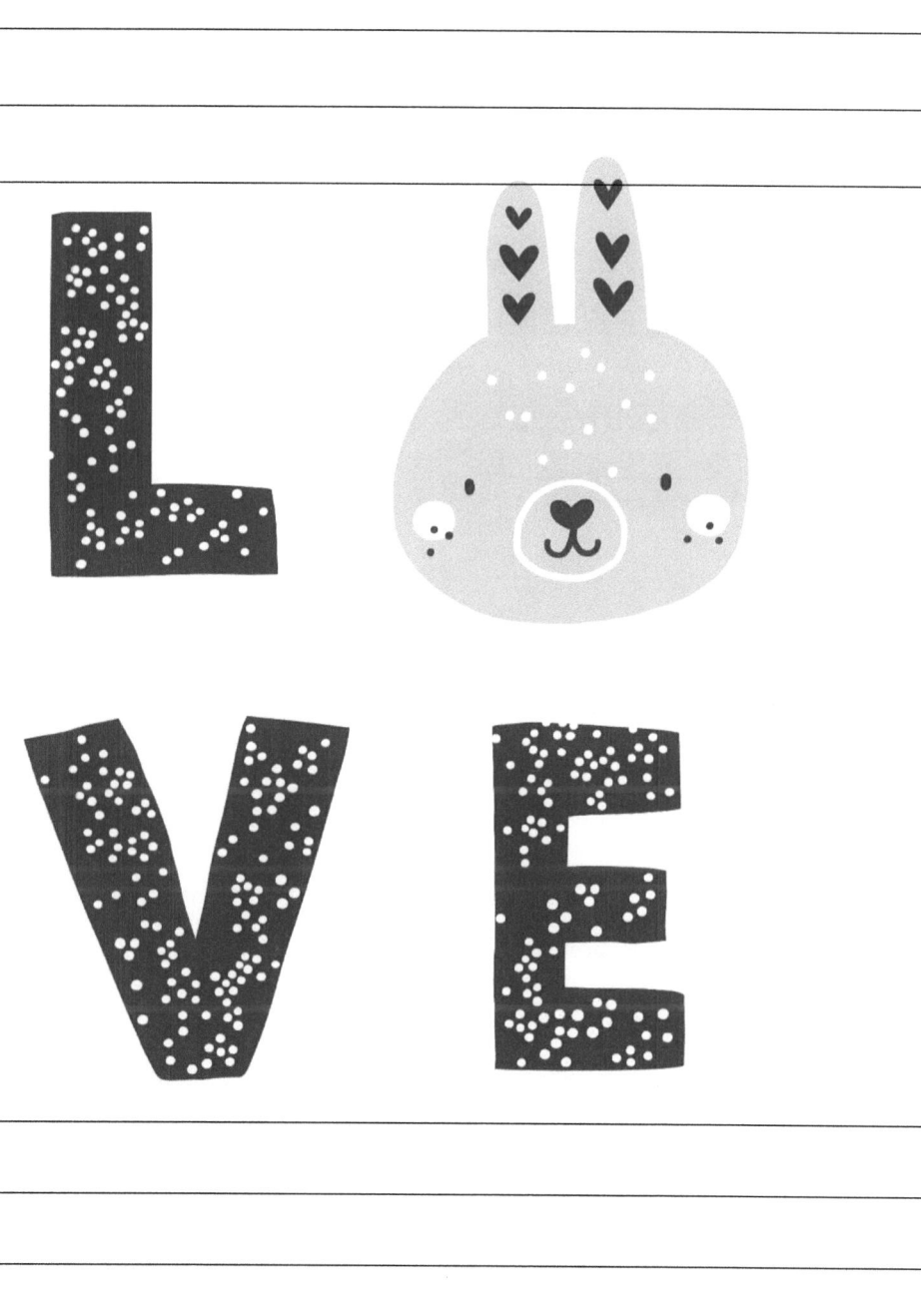

12 Months Old

Date: _____

Likes

Feedings:

Sleep Patterns:

(Picture)

Weight: _____

Height: _____

Dislikes

Head Circumference: _____

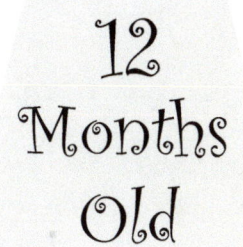

12 Months Old

Milestones

Milestone Achieved	Yes	No
Responds To Simple Requests		
Waves Hello Or Goodbye		
May Start Using Basic Words		
Acknowledges Objects When Named		
Can Stand Alone		
Sleeps Through The Night		
May Start Responding To Music		

Comments

_____
_____
_____
_____
_____

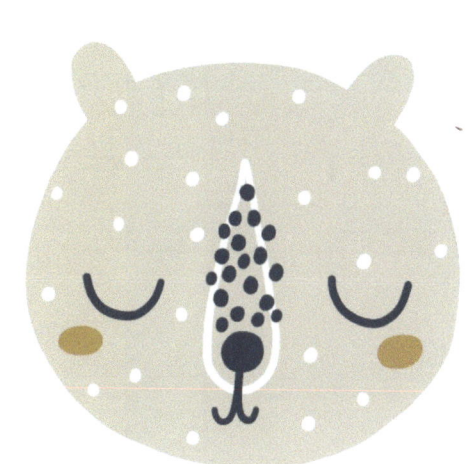

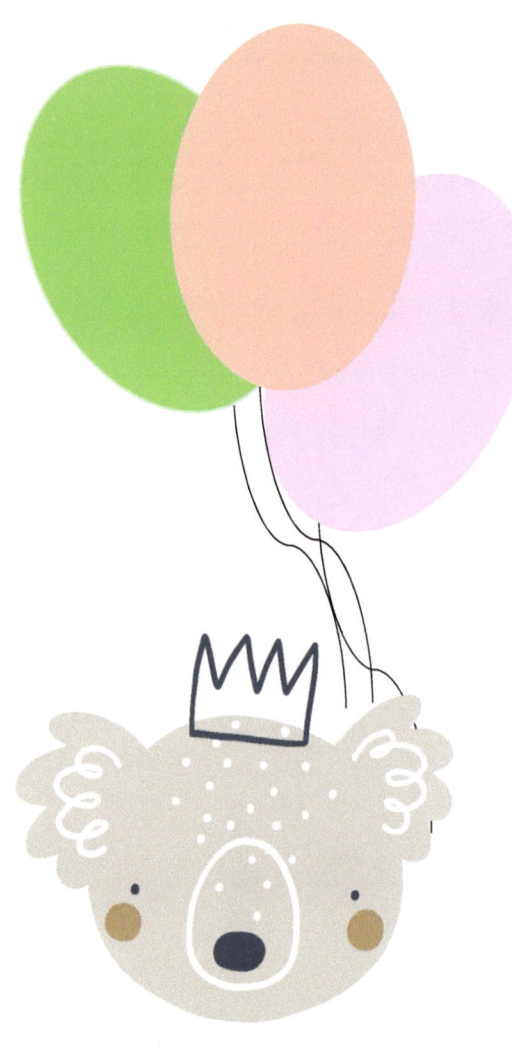

Happy Birthday

All About My First Birthday

_____
_____
_____
_____
_____
_____
_____
_____

(Picture)

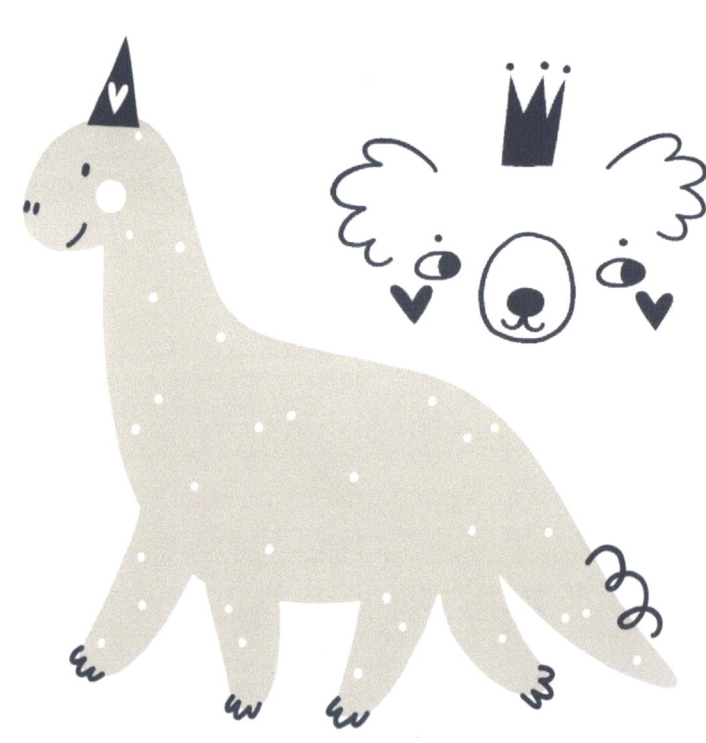

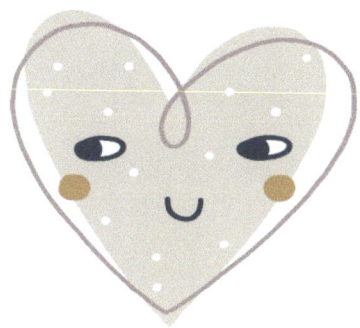 # Personality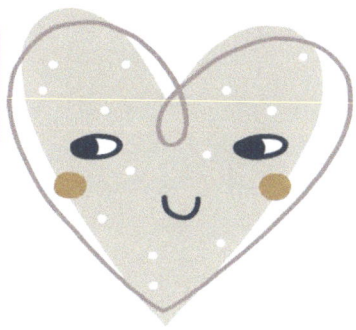

Mothers Opinion:

_____
_____
_____
_____
_____
_____

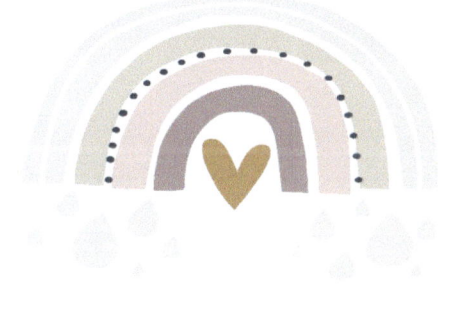 ## Fathers Opinion: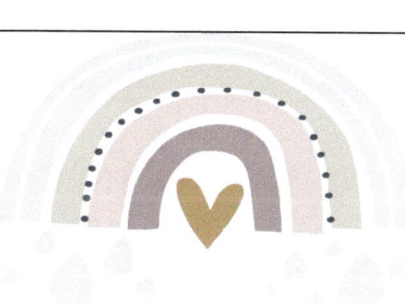

_____
_____
_____
_____
_____
_____

My First Christmas

Gifts Received

_____
_____
_____
_____
_____
_____

(Picture)

Who Was There?

_____
_____
_____
_____
_____
_____

Thoughts

_____
_____
_____
_____
_____
_____

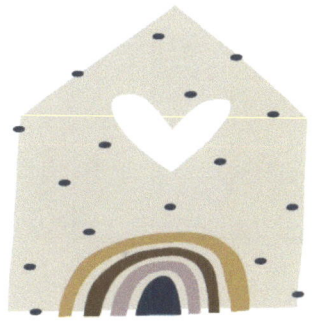
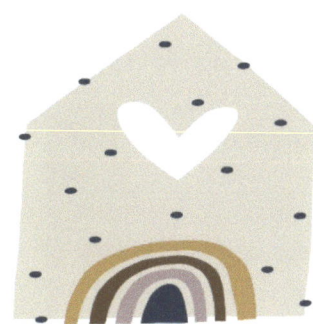

Firsts

Address Of First Home:

First Smile:

First Doctor Visit:

First Laugh:

First Time I Rolled Over:

First Time I Crawled:

First Solid Food:

First Time I reached For An Object:

First Time I Sat Up Without Aid:

First Time I Stood Up:

First Steps:

My First Words:

First Tooth:

First Haircut:

Thoughts

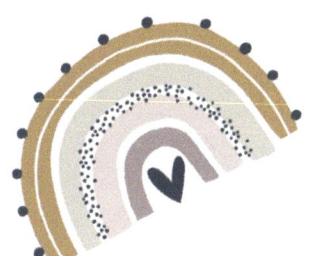

Family Pictures

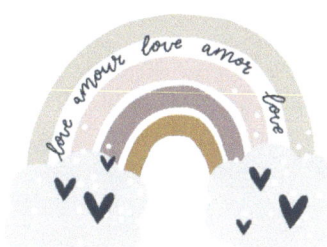

(Picture)

(Picture)

(Picture)

(Picture)

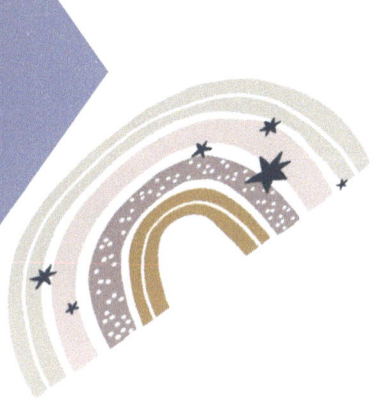

(Picture)

Family Pictures

(Picture)

(Picture)

(Picture)

(Picture)

(Picture)

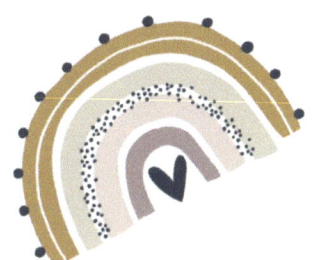

Family Pictures

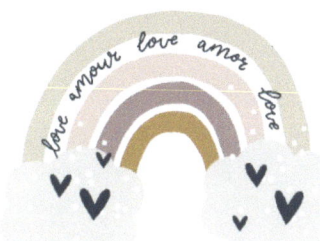

(Picture)

(Picture)

(Picture)

(Picture)

(Picture)

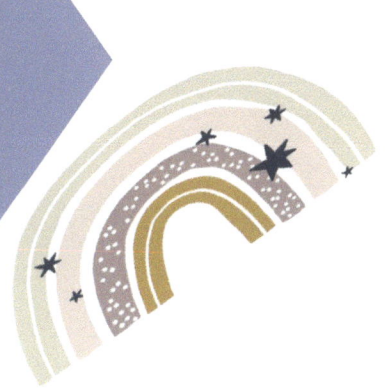

(Picture)